Animals with Jobs

Carrier Pigeons

Judith Janda Presnall

KIDHAVEN
PRESS™

THOMSON
━━━━✦━━━━™
GALE

San Diego • Detroit • New York • San Francisco • Cleveland
New Haven, Conn. • Waterville, Maine • London • Munich

For Kaye & Kory

For more information, contact
KidHaven Press
27500 Drake Rd.
Farmington Hills, MI 48331-3535
Or you can visit our Internet site at http://www.gale.com

LIBRARY OF CONGRESS CATALOGING-IN-PUBLICATION DATA

Presnall, Judith Janda.
  Carrier pigeons / by Judith Janda Presnall.
    p. cm. — (Animals with jobs)
Summary: Discusses the types of pigeons used for carrying messages and their use in wartime.
Includes bibliographical references (p.   ).
  ISBN 0-7377-1824-2 (hardback : alk. paper)
  1. Homing pigeons—Juvenile literature. [1. Homing pigeons. 2. Pigeons.]
  I. Title. II. Series.
  UH90.P74 2004
  358'.24—dc21

                       2003000882

Contents

Chapter One

Airborne Messengers

In their jobs, **carrier** pigeons have helped people in remarkable ways for over three thousand years. The birds have carried messages, delivered blood samples, and even transported film **cartridges.** Their greatest contribution occurred during World Wars I and II when they flew over battlefields to deliver important messages to soldiers. Until recently, pigeons aided **communications** between remote police stations in underdeveloped areas that lacked **telegraphs** and telephones.

Why Use Pigeons?

A pigeon's most important characteristic is its ability to home, or return to the place it was raised. The pigeon's destination is its home. People take the pigeons with them in the field, to an island, on a ship or airplane, or leave them at someone's house. When released, the bird flies home. This ability is still a puzzle. People have studied the pigeon for centuries, trying to understand the bird's natural **homing** ability. "Scientists don't know. Nobody knows how they do it. It's a mystery,"[1] says Bob Dettlinger, a pigeon enthusiast in Etna, Pennsylvania.

Several explanations have been suggested. For instance, pigeons may possess an inner drive to return home that is similar to a bird's instinct to build a nest or

Scientists study the homing ability of pigeons. No one knows why pigeons always return home.

Scientists place a compass on a pigeon's back to study the bird's homing ability.

feed its young. Or the birds may come home because they know food is there and they want to return to their mates. Some scientists think that pigeons find their way home by using the Earth's **magnetic** fields. This means that their brains work like a compass to figure out north, south, east, and west.

Proof of Skill

People have tested the pigeon's remarkable homing ability. In the 1960s, a group of French pigeon **fanciers** decided to test a pigeon to see if he could find his way home from over seven thousand miles away. The gray bird was shipped from his loft in Saigon in a covered basket. For many weeks, he was stowed in the dark hold of a ship, which sailed through the Red Sea and the Mediterranean.

The pigeon never saw land and could not have memorized landmarks or shorelines. He was taken to a **loft** in Arras, France. There, he was fed and given time to recover from his confinement. Then the French pigeon fanciers tossed him aloft for his trip home. The pigeon found his home shed in twenty-five days. The bird had only lost one ounce after flying seventy-two hundred miles. This pigeon's home-finding trip perplexed many people. But it proved the unusual ability of a homing pigeon.

Characteristics of Pigeons

Pigeons exhibit a number of traits that make them useful for delivering messages. They are fast. Pigeons fly at the rate of about a mile a minute—as fast as a car could travel. Unlike cars, however, pigeons can take a more direct route.

Pigeons adapt well to various weather or terrain. If it is foggy, they fly above the fog. In mountainous areas, pigeons swoop into valleys, where they meet less wind resistance. And pigeons are reliable. They return to their home loft 95 percent of the time.

Pigeons adapt to foggy weather by flying above the clouds.

The First Carrier Pigeons

Throughout history, pigeons have been used in different ways. The ancient Greeks used homing pigeons to report results of the Olympic Games. In the fifth and sixth centuries B.C., representatives from each province took pigeons to the games so they could send word back home

Women release a carrier pigeon with the results of a sailboat race in this nineteenth-century drawing.

Before the invention of the telegraph, reporters like these sent their stories by carrier pigeon.

as to how the local boys were doing. The pigeon messengers had tiny capsules attached to their legs with the results written on a small paper inside the capsule.

In the days of the pharaohs, when navigators sailing to Egypt saw land, they would release pigeons with a message notifying their families that they would soon be home.

The military branches—army, navy, and air force—found pigeons useful as message carriers, too. Until the invention of the telegraph in 1837 and the telephone in 1876, the fastest way to send any kind of news was by pigeon.

Dangerous Jobs: Military Pigeons

Many pigeons lost their lives serving in the military. If enemy soldiers were nearby when a pigeon was released, they tried to shoot the bird down. They knew the pigeon was carrying an important message to the other side. In a war between France and Prussia in 1870, Prussians turned flocks of hawks loose to attack the birds.

During the two world wars, carrier pigeons substituted for two-way radios. When officials did not want to send a radio message for fear that the enemy would hear it, pigeons were a safe alternative. They were also useful when a radio was out of commission or when the location would not allow for radio use.

Pigeons carry news photos in capsules on their backs.

HE SCOTSMAN — DAILY EXPRESS — REUTER — DAILY TELEGRAPH — DAILY MAIL

PARK YOUR PIGEONS HERE

A press center on a golf course in Scotland offers boxes for the pigeons of each newspaper.

Safe Work: Pigeons Work for the Newspapers

In the 1940s, pigeons played a role in the Newspaper Enterprise Association (NEA), a news service. Like today, newspapers competed against each other to be the first to print up-to-the-minute news and photographs. When a ship approached the New York harbor, famous people would often be aboard. The NEA reporters carried pigeons in a small boat out to the ship.

On board, the NEA reporters photographed famous people and political dignitaries. The negatives were put into capsules that were harnessed onto the backs of the birds. The pigeons were then released. They reached their home, the NEA office, within a few minutes. The film was quickly developed, and newspapers were printed within two hours, thereby beating out the competing newspapers. By the time the ship finally docked, NEA newspapers were already being sold on New York streets.

Pigeons in the 1980s

In Florida in 1987, a *Jacksonville Journal* photographer cleverly outsmarted fellow photographers. He had brought his homing pigeon on an assignment to a memorial service for sailors. President Ronald Reagan and his wife, Nancy, attended this service to honor those who had died in an attack on the *USS Stark.* The reporter snapped photos of the service and had his pigeon deliver the film to his newspaper within an hour. He had scooped the rest of the photographers who, for security reasons, were detained at the naval station.

Pigeons have proven reliable and fast **couriers.** But first, in order to learn their trade, they must be given extensive training.

Chapter Two

Training

When the United States entered World War I in 1917, American military leaders were eager to enlist men who had experience in handling and training homing pigeons. The Army's **pigeoneer** men trained thousands of pigeons for active service. At one time, every army camp in the United States had a government bird loft. During World War II, the U.S. Army employed more than three thousand soldiers who managed fifty-four thousand pigeons throughout Asia, North Africa, and Europe.

Until 1962, the U.S. Army Signal Corps at Fort Monmouth, New Jersey, bred and trained pigeons for all the military branches in the United States. In addition, civilian pigeon fanciers gave their own homing pigeons to the military.

The Pigeon Corps
A carrier pigeon's main job is to make a delivery to its home loft. Upon landing, pigeons enter a one-way trap

13

Pigeoneers are experienced in handling and training homing pigeons.

door that is wired to sound a bell or buzzer. This alerts the person on duty at the loft that a message has arrived.

Pigeons that worked for the military began their training at four to five weeks of age. The tiny birds were called squeakers. Even before they were able to fly, trainers placed the squeakers on the roof of their loft every day, helping the birds to become accustomed to their surroundings.

When the squeakers grew stronger, trainers moved them a few feet away from their loft and then encouraged them to fly back. The birds were also trained to enter the loft when called. Trainers accomplished this by repeating a sound, such as whistling or shaking a food can, at feeding time. The birds soon learned to associate certain sounds with food and would respond by returning to the loft. Pigeons were not fed before a training session or a mission. This encouraged them to return home for food.

At the age of eight weeks, all the pigeons were allowed to exercise by flying in wide circles over their loft twice a day. These sessions lasted one hour. During the following month, the pigeons learned to adjust to the small, uncomfortable wicker baskets that would be used to transport them from place to place.

Pigeon chicks, called squeakers, begin their homing training when they are four to five weeks old.

Group Training

For the pigeons' first distance test, they were transported in baskets five miles from their loft, bumping and jostling against each other. At their destination, the trainers released the flock all together. When released, the birds flew straight up, then circled until their mysterious direction finder set them on a straight line toward home.

Dogs often transported carrier pigeon baskets during World War I.

Pigeons learned to find their home loft, even when it was moved every day.

Day after day, week after week, this process continued with the birds being released farther from home. Trainers released them from points north, south, east, and west. This taught the pigeons to find their home loft when approaching from any direction.

During early training, the pigeons' loft was moved every day so the birds became accustomed to looking for it. Their movable loft, a converted house trailer, became their permanent home. The signal corps had fifty of these specially designed mobile lofts, each housing 140 pigeons.

Advanced Training

As the pigeons' military training advanced, the trainers kept increasing the flying distances from their lofts. For example, on one mission they might fly 10 miles, but on the next flight the distance would be raised to 15 miles. The trainers kept boosting the mileage until finally the pigeons were taken about 125 miles away from their lofts. Some pigeons showed great **stamina** and were able to endure these longer missions. Other pigeons were swifter and better suited for shorter trips.

Once the groups of pigeons were able to return to their lofts from fifty miles away, trainers released the birds singly at shorter distances in order to accustom them to flying alone. Weak pigeons were eliminated from the training program. Those pigeons that stopped to rest in trees or on telephone wires were also eliminated. On the job, reliable pigeons stay in the air from sunrise to sunset and do not stop to eat, drink, or rest.

Training continued until the pigeons were seven months old. In their final test, the birds were taken about fifty miles out to sea aboard a ship or an airplane and released. They were expected to head straight for land and reach their loft in the shortest possible time.

Adjustments for Military Pigeons

In addition to finding its home, a carrier pigeon had to adapt to having a message capsule attached to its leg or back. For larger items such as photographic film, multiple messages, or maps, the pigeon wore a harness. The harness fit over the shoulders, under the wings, and

Carrier pigeons carried some loads in capsules attached to their backs.

across the breast, and it had two elastic loops on the top for the tube. Loads weighing up to three ounces could be carried in the tube that balanced on the bird's back.

Night Flyers

Pigeons had **supplementary** training if they needed to fly at night. It is generally accepted that a pigeon's rapid and safe return to its loft is determined by daylight and by visibility. Most pigeons will not fly in the dark unless they are very near home. If darkness overtakes pigeons while they are flying, they will rest during the night and continue their journey the next morning.

Thomas Ross, chief pigeon expert for the army, selected a dozen squeakers as candidates for his night-flying squad. These squeakers were the result of breeding two kinds of pigeons: those that demonstrated an unusual fondness for the dark and those that had a strong sense of direction. Ross settled these twelve pigeons into a special loft. He explained his training procedure:

All day long the birds were kept inside their loft. A little reflected sunlight was all they ever saw. After sundown, I'd let them out for exercise, and they'd flutter around and try their wings. Every week I'd make this daily exercise period a little later in the twilight, until finally they were working wholly in the dark.

Then, one evening, I took them out, carried them 100 yards away and released them. My helper stayed in the loft and rattled the food can, and the hungry birds hurried home for supper.[2]

Ross gradually increased the flying distance. He discovered that the pigeons did not fly well in moonlight. The night flyers performed best in complete darkness. The average flight mileage of night flyers eventually increased to twenty miles. Night flyers were valuable because it was easier for them to escape hawks or enemy bullets.

Two-Way War Birds

The most dramatic achievement of the army pigeoneers was that of training two-way war birds. These special birds were used to carry messages between frontline troops and headquarters. Since birds want to drink after feeding, the army provided a feeding station at one loft and water at the other loft. A soldier attached a message to a pigeon. The hungry bird flew to its destination at headquarters, had the tube emptied and refilled with another message, ate, and then flew back to drink at its second loft at the front line. This allowed the army to receive and send messages using the same pigeon.

Pigeons have experienced many on-the-job adventures in the armed services, demonstrating proof of their intelligence and special homing ability.

Two-way war birds were trained using their habit of drinking after feeding.

Chapter Three

Birds of War

Pigeons performed extraordinary work during wartime. They completed millions of deliveries. One pigeon alone, named The Mocker, flew fifty-two missions before he was wounded. Numerous birds were recognized with awards, medals, and plaques in appreciation of their dedicated service.

War Use

Pigeons were helpful messengers during the Franco-Prussian War of 1870. After the Prussians encircled the city of Paris, the French used pigeons to communicate with the troops as well as friends and relatives. Authorities set up a pigeon dispatch center in Tours, France. At the center, people tacked hundreds of personal messages on boards. The letters were photographically reduced onto microfilm.

This process made it possible for each bird to carry a cartridge of three thousand messages. Some strong fliers

World War I pigeoneers attach a message to the leg of a carrier pigeon.

could carry five and six cartridges at one time. When cartridges were received at the post office, each message was remagnified by a special projector and cast on a screen. It was then copied by a postal clerk and delivered to the intended person in standard, readable form.

During the five months of fighting in Paris, courier pigeons are said to have delivered one hundred thousand official military messages and more than 1 million letters to private citizens between Tours and Paris.

World War I Hero Pigeon: Cher Ami

Of the six hundred birds donated by the British Pigeon Service for use in World War I, the most famous was a carrier pigeon named Cher Ami (French for "Dear Friend"). Cher Ami's twelfth and final mission was in the Argonne Forest of France. A group of over five hundred American soldiers, who had become separated from their 77th Infantry Division, were lost in the Argonne Forest. This group, which came to be known as the Lost **Battalion,** had six carrier pigeons with them.

Enemy German soldiers had surrounded the lost American soldiers and killed or wounded three hundred on the first day. The rest of the 77th Division, not knowing the location of their lost battalion, mistook them for Germans and began dropping bombs on them. In order to keep from being killed by their own army, members of the Lost Battalion began releasing a pigeon each day, hoping to inform the American commanders of their location and predicament.

A British Army unit releases a carrier pigeon with an important message.

Major Charles W. Whittlesey sent the first pigeon out with a note that read: "We are being shelled by German artillery. Can we not have artillery support?"[3]

The next day, a second pigeon was released with this plea: "Situation very serious. Have not been able to re-establish runner posts. Need ammunition."[4]

On the third day, food and water were running short. Whittlesey sent out pigeon number three with this information: "Our posts are broken, one runner captured.

Germans in small numbers in our left rear. Have located German mortar [a muzzle-loading cannon] and have sent platoon to get it. E Company met heavy resistance—at least 20 casualties."[5]

A fourth pigeon brought news of the past two days' casualties—9 killed and 140 wounded.

But German sharpshooters and machine gunners brought down bird after bird. The sergeant who handled the pigeons was weak with exhaustion and trembled when the fifth pigeon was released. His fumbling caused the bird to flutter away before the message could be inserted into its leg tube. The only pigeon left was Cher Ami.

Wounded Cher Ami Fights Back

With a message safely in his leg tube, Cher Ami flew toward home. When a bullet tore out an eye, the stunned pigeon tumbled toward the earth. The semiconscious bird next was hit in the breastbone. But his instinct to fly home motivated him to fight back. Cher Ami was next struck in the leg, but he managed to stretch his wings and climb higher and higher, beyond the reach of enemy guns.

The battalion's hopes soared! The bird, soaked in blood, flew twenty-five miles to his home loft. The precious message capsule was still attached, dangling from the ligaments of his shattered leg.

The message read: "We are along the road parallel 276.4. Our own artillery is dropping a barrage directly on us. For heaven's sake stop it."[6]

Cher Ami's heroic flight resulted in the rescue of two hundred exhausted soldiers. After medics patched up his wounds, Cher Ami lived eight months longer. Cher Ami's preserved body is on display at the National Museum of American History, Smithsonian Institution, in Washington, D.C. For his brave action under fire,

Carrier pigeon Cher Ami was awarded the Croix de Guerre.

the French government awarded Cher Ami with the Croix de Guerre. This is a special medal recognizing heroism in battle.

Navy Couriers

Often the pigeons' home lofts were moved to different locations, as was the case with the British Royal Navy. Baskets of pigeons were placed aboard all British **trawlers.** In one incident, a German submarine had attacked the trawler *Nelson*. The captain had been badly wounded by gunfire. Crawling across the deck to the pigeon basket, he attached a message to a pigeon named Crisp. Crisp had to find his home loft, now aboard a ship that changed its **moorings** every few days. Crisp skillfully located the navy ship before nightfall and delivered the news that the *Nelson* was in trouble. The damaged trawler was found, and every sailor rescued.

During World War II, another gallant pigeon named Winkie earned a plaque for a sea rescue. This pigeon flew one hundred miles to save a crew of four British Air Force men whose bomber aircraft had crashed into the North Sea. The impact of the wreck had opened the pigeon cage. While the crew floated in a yellow **dinghy,** Winkie flew with wet, oil-stained wings to her Scotland home loft. Even though she did not have a message attached to her, Winkie's owner, James Ross, reported her return. He called the British Operations with her leg code number, and it was traced to a specific aircraft. Within an hour, the downed men were rescued.

World War II: Air Force

Besides working for the army and navy, some pigeons had jobs with the air force, which required a different kind of performance. When released from a plane, the pigeons had to learn to "dead drop," or plummet, through the plane's slipstream, which is the rapid airflow around and behind the aircraft. Until they learned to keep their wings tucked close to their bodies, inexperienced birds whirled helplessly in the slipstream. If they survived, the confused, dizzy birds usually took longer to set their course before heading home. Obviously, something had to be done.

An American serviceman soon developed a safer method of releasing pigeons from aircraft. Airmen dropped the birds through a release hatch in ordinary grocery bags that had been slit on one side. The bag protected the bird as it dropped through the slipstream of the propellers. As soon as the bag cleared the turbulent wind, it opened wide and blew away. The pigeon then flew off on its mission.

British troops attach messages to carrier pigeons during World War II.

This kind of training was important in case a pilot lost radio contact or a damaged plane was in danger of crashing. In this situation, an airman released pigeons to notify ground rescuers at the base.

World War II Heroes

During World War II, thirty-one wartime pigeons received the Dickin Medal for valor, which is awarded to heroic animals that serve humans. One of these birds was G.I. Joe. He is credited with saving a British **brigade** of one thousand soldiers serving in Italy. The U.S. Army Air Force had been ordered to bomb an Italian village, Colvi Vecchia, thought to be under German control. But the British had already advanced into the area. They tried to notify the Americans that they had taken the city, but all radio and other communication attempts had failed.

A British soldier prepares to release a homing pigeon from an airplane.

British pigeoneers hurried to release G.I. Joe with a message to the Americans to call off the bombing. The bird flew twenty miles in twenty minutes through enemy artillery fire and arrived at the U.S. Air Support Command base just as pilots were warming up their planes to take off. This speedy delivery of the message by G.I. Joe stopped the Americans from bombing their British allies.

Pigeons' military careers were short-lived. Other, faster forms of communication and electronic devices eventually replaced the birds. The U.S. Army Signal Corps at Fort Monmouth, New Jersey, closed down its military pigeon training facility in 1962. The remaining birds were donated to public zoos and zoological gardens throughout the United States.

Chapter Four

Pigeons in Peacetime

Homing pigeons perform gallantly in peacetime as well. Doctors and police in remote areas, where communication by radio or telephone is impossible, use pigeons to send and receive urgent messages. Pigeons also carry messages of hope during catastrophes.

Police Pigeon Service

When World War II ended in 1945, the U.S. Army returned over nine thousand birds to the civilian pigeon fanciers who had owned them before the war. Another eight hundred pigeons were delivered to police stations in poverty-stricken Orissa in eastern India. These stations were remote and far apart. There was no money for radio or telephone links. For half a century, the Police Pigeon Service used the birds to carry vital messages between villages and towns.

The police wrote messages on a scrap of paper, rolled it up, and inserted it into a tiny plastic capsule that was then attached to a pigeon's leg with a rubber band. One message sent from the Central Breeding and Headquarter loft in the city of Cuttack read: "Report immediately to HQ about the incident at Gurudijhati . . . in which two persons were killed in violence. Send a constable with all details."[7]

Pigeons also proved invaluable when disasters, such as floods and cyclones, made communication networks unusable in Orissa. The pigeons saved the day after a cyclone tore into the region on October 29, 1999, killing 8,495 people and snapping communication links with coastal areas. However, even in remote India, technology

The Police Pigeon Service allows small villages and towns in India to communicate with each other.

advanced enough to make the Police Pigeon Service become obsolete. The police have since transferred the pigeons to the state's wildlife department.

Medical Messenger Service

Carrier pigeons continue to serve the medical needs of doctors in France. The small island of Yeu off the coast of France in the Bay of Biscay has no medical laboratory. When a blood sample needs to be analyzed, it is placed in a red fluorescent pouch and strapped to a homing pigeon's belly. The bird flies thirty-two miles to its loft in the mainland town of Les Sables-d'Olonne.

An ambulance driver meets the pigeon at its loft, removes the sample, and transports it to the hospital. Lab technicians run tests and then telephone the results to the doctor on Yeu. For safety, two samples are collected. If the pigeon has not arrived at the loft in Les Sables-d'Olonne after two hours, the second blood sample is sent.

A helicopter takes an hour to complete this trip, but a pigeon makes it in twenty-five minutes. During winter months, only one or two pigeons fly to the mainland each day. However, during the summer tourist season, when Yeu's population of five thousand triples, as many as six birds may fly daily.

Doctors and Pharmacists Use Pigeon Carriers

Throughout history, the amazing homing ability of these swift birds has been used in fascinating ways. About a

In isolated rural communities, people kept carrier pigeons to send messages.

century ago, when telephones were rare in the isolated farming communities of Pennsylvania, one doctor had a small loft built next to his office. He left a pigeon at most of his patients' farms. When an emergency arose and a family needed the doctor, they inserted a message into the bird's capsule and sent it off. The bird flew to the doctor's loft. When the doctor made the house call, he left another pigeon at the farm.

A country pharmacist, Julio Hael, in Buenos Aires, Argentina, also used pigeon carriers. The pigeon service was for customers within a twenty-mile radius of his pharmacy. Hael began a pigeon center and gave each of his customers lacking a telephone a pigeon. When medicines were needed, the customer wrote the order on a piece of paper and slipped it into the container on the bird's leg. Minutes later, the bird arrived at Hael's **cote.** The medicine was delivered at once by someone from the pharmacy, and a new pigeon was left with the customer. Each of Hael's pigeons made about two hundred trips a year.

Carrier Pigeons Served During Floods

Pigeons also were valuable during floods when all wires were destroyed, knocking out radio communication. In 1936, ravaging floods completely submerged most of the Midwest. A writer describes how pigeons helped:

> Airplanes scouted the regions and lowered pigeons to stranded people. They in turn attached messages to the birds stating their most immediate food and medical requirements. In a short time the birds delivered the message and the rescuers were enabled to set forth with the needed supplies.[8]

Young pigeoneers like this one often train their birds to compete in races.

Pigeon Express

Pigeons also help people make money. Dave Costlow, owner of Rocky Mountain Adventures, has increased his souvenir profits by employing pigeons. He runs rafting excursions down the Cache la Poudre River in Colorado.

Each morning a Rocky Mountain Adventures photographer arrives at a riverside location with a camera and a cage holding up to ten homing pigeons.

When the photographer sights the paddling white-water rafters, he frantically snaps a roll of film of them hurtling down the river. The photographer then places the film into a pigeon's tiny, custom-tailored lycra backpack and launches the bird into the air. The bird flies twenty miles to its home loft at Costlow's store, where an employee develops the film. By the time the rafters complete their trip, the keepsake photos are ready for purchase.

Although a roll of film may get lost occasionally, the birds are never sick and are always on time. On their trip, the birds must fly fast enough to outmaneuver the peregrine falcons roaming the sky. One year, Costlow lost three pigeons to hawks.

Costlow is familiar with the habits of his pigeons. This helps him better utilize their services. Costlow gives an example: "Pigeons mate for life, so we only fly one member of the couple on any trip. That way they hustle back home. Let the couple go together and they dilly dally."[9]

Birds from Rocky Mountain Adventures Pigeon Express use lycra backpacks to carry film.

Pigeoneers are always ready to volunteer their birds to help in emergencies.

When birds grow too old to fly distances, they can be used for breeding in their retirement years.

Today, a few pigeons have jobs, but most of them have been replaced with faster forms of communication. However, when an emergency arises, the racing pigeon fanciers are able and willing to supply the winged messengers to the Red Cross and Civil Defense Organizations wherever they are needed.

Notes

Chapter One: Airborne Messengers

1. Quoted in Brandon Keat, "Pigeons Ready to Race, Serve If Needed," *Pittsburgh Tribune-Review*, July 23, 2002, p. 2.

Chapter Two: Training

2. Quoted in George W. Gray, "Uncle Sam's Fly-By-Nights," *Popular Mechanics*, December 1931, p. 955.

Chapter Three: Birds of War

3. Arch Whitehouse, *Heroic Pigeons*, New York, G.P. Putnam's Sons, 1965, p. 64.

4. Whitehouse, *Heroic Pigeons*, p. 65.

5. Whitehouse, *Heroic Pigeons*, p. 65.

6. Whitehouse, *Heroic Pigeons*, p. 67.

Chapter Four: Pigeons in Peacetime

7. Quoted in Pawel Kopczynski, "Pigeon 911," *Washington Post*, November 27, 2000.

8. Belle Ross, "Nature's Aerial Couriers," *Travel*, January 1941, p. 18.

9. Quoted in Bijal P. Trivedi, "Pigeons on the Payroll," *National Geographic Today*, August 15, 2001. p. 3.

Glossary

battalion: A skilled, organized military unit.

brigade: A military unit composed of combat battalions.

carrier: One that carries or transports messages or goods.

cartridges: Tubular cases.

communications: The exchange of thoughts, messages, or information.

cote: A small shed or shelter for birds.

courier: A messenger on urgent or official business.

dinghy: A small rowboat.

fanciers: People who have a special enthusiasm in raising a specific kind of plant or animal.

homing: Going or returning home.

loft: A shelter for pigeons.

magnetic: Relating to the magnetic poles of the Earth.

moorings: Places where a vessel can be anchored.

pigeoneer: A person who works with pigeons.

stamina: Physical power of endurance.

supplementary: Something added.

telegraphs: Messages sent by a communication system that is connected by wires; the machine transmits and receives messages.

trawlers: Boats used for catching fish by dragging nets along the sea bottom.

Organizations to Contact

American Racing Pigeon Union
PO Box 18465
Oklahoma City, OK 73154-0465
(405) 848-5801
www.pigeon.org
This site has information for hobbyists as well as those interested in the sporting approach of racing. Basic topics include the birds, the loft, nutrition, general care and management, training, health, breeding, clubs, and competition.

The National Pigeon Association
NPA Junior Program
Phil Harper
202 Sharon Lane
Montgomery, AL 36108
(334) 269-2039
www.npausa.com
This site has information for young people interested in raising, breeding, and racing pigeons. It also contains a newsletter with informative articles.

For Further Exploration

Books

Ray Nofsinger and Jim Hargrove, *Pigeons and Doves*. Chicago: Childrens Press, 1992. This book is an introduction to pigeons. It discusses physical characteristics, talents of homing pigeons, and pet care.

Dorothy Hinshaw Patent, *Pigeons*. New York: Clarion Books, 1997. This book reports the physical characteristics, behavior, and usefulness of pigeons, which have dwelled with people since prehistoric times.

Miriam Schlein, *Pigeons*. New York: Thomas Y. Crowell, 1989. This book explains how pigeons—descendants of wild rock doves—live their lives, raise their young, and have been useful throughout history to people.

Video

Huell Howser, *California's Gold*, "Wings Over California," 1994. (Produced by Huell Howser Productions in association with KCET-TV.) Howser takes viewers to Avalon on Catalina Island, to the site of the Pigeon Courier Service. Owned and operated by the Zahn brothers from 1894–1897, this company delivered messages between the mainland and Catalina.

Index

Picture Credits

About the Author

Judith Janda Presnall is an award-winning nonfiction writer. *Carrier Pigeons* is the ninth book in the series of Animals with Jobs. Her other books include *Rachel Carson, Artificial Organs, The Giant Panda, Oprah Winfrey, Mount Rushmore, Life on Alcatraz, Animals That Glow, Animal Skeletons,* and *Circuses.* Presnall graduated from the University of Wisconsin in Whitewater. She is a recipient of the Jack London Award for meritorious service in the California Writers Club. She is also a member of the Society of Children's Book Writers and Illustrators. Judith lives in the Los Angeles area with her husband, Lance, and three cats.